Percy's Quest

Barbara Follows
Illustrated by Penelope Follows

TSL Publications

First published in Great Britain in 2023
By TSL Publications, Rickmansworth

Copyright © 2023 Barbara Follows

ISBN: 978-1-915660-40-4

The right of Barbara Follows to be identified as the author and Penelope Follows as the illustrator of this work has been asserted by the author in accordance with the UK Copyright, Designs and Patents Act 1988.

All characters and events in this publication, other than those clearly in the public domain, are fictitious and any resemblance to actual persons, living or dead, is purely coincidental.

All rights reserved. No part of this publication may be reproduced, stored in a retrieval system or transmitted, in any form or by any means without the prior written permission of the publisher, nor be otherwise circulated in any form of binding or cover other than that in which it is published and without a similar condition being imposed on the subsequent buyer.

Cover courtesy of : Penelope Follows

For Lilly Barbara Follows

With special thanks to 'Penny' Follows,
Peter Follows, Year 5 pupils 2021–2022,
Lyndhurst School, Camberley
and the support of Bodil Marie Sørensen.

Plus, a dedication to 'Tinker' who died of old age
during the publication of this story and to
'Hedgley' who sadly did not.

Contents

		Page
The Beginning		7
1	Henry	8
2	Percy and Henry	15
3	The Refrigerator	20
4	The Garden	24
5	Corey	28
6	The Christmas Tree Plantation	33
7	Holly and Tinker	37
8	Hedgley	41
9	Hazel	48
10	Goodbyes	54
11	The Oak Trees	58
12	Chief	62
13	The Lake	68
14	The Storm	73
15	The Ending	79

The Beginning

The tree was shaking so hard that Percy, a young tree rat, was thrown out of his bed and flung through the air down into a bush. Terrified and bewildered, he could only stare in shock, as he watched the tree that he had been sleeping in with his family, being taken away on the back of a lorry. He called and searched for his parents and his brothers and sisters. But no one answered back. Where were the rest of his family? Percy's quest to find them was about to begin and it begins with Henry.

1. Henry

Henry, a little field mouse, had been forced to leave the family nest and was awfully sad, as he had enjoyed living with his younger brothers and sisters. His other siblings had left home a few weeks before. But he didn't feel as confident as them. His mum and dad, although strict, had made him feel safe and cared for. He still loves his family and can't understand why his parents have now sent him out into the world before he feels ready. He doesn't chirp any more, as there is no one to play or have fun with. His parents said that he was too fastidious (he had to look that word up) and too sensitive. They told him that for his own good he had to leave home and look after himself. That way, he would become stronger, more independent and not so reliant on his sisters. He doesn't understand that last bit as he loved playing with them, much more than with his brothers whose boisterous games always seemed to end up with shoving and fighting. In particular, he liked helping to prepare meals for his family. But now he was on his own, confused and lonely.

Henry spent his nights walking, looking for a new home and foraging for food. It was exceptionally scary trying to keep safe. In fact, the worst time of Henry's short life. He had to find places to hide and sleep during the day. One of these was a barn where he snuggled down into the straw and cried himself to sleep. That evening he scuttled out of the barn and across a field where he could smell that the farm cat had been hunting. He didn't want to be hunted, so he stopped often to sniff the air for any danger and to twitch his whiskers, deciding which way to go. Henry crossed field after field, pushing his way through dense undergrowth and avoiding being stomped on by cows. He was becoming rather tired when he was surprised by a flat, black field ahead with bright flashing lights and rumbling noises that came and went. Henry took a deep breath and ploughed ahead as quickly as he could, avoiding the monster wheels that threatened to flatten him. He fell into a ditch on the other side, landing on his back looking up at the stars and a large white shape that appeared to be swooping down … for him! He curled into a ball, rolled under some leaves and waited for the talons of the owl to grab him. 'Swoosh' went the owl's wings, 'swoosh' and away from Henry. The little mouse closed his eyes and exhausted, fell asleep.

The next morning Henry woke up wondering where on earth he was. He was alarmed and disorientated, as normally he slept during the day. But he was still very, very tired, so he pushed the leaves to one side and dug and dug until he had made a cosy burrow. The next time he woke, the sun was dipping down out of sight and Henry realised that he was very, very hungry and very, very thirsty. He scuttled along through the trees, crossing a meadow and twitching his nose for smells, being exceedingly careful of any more owls. He was relieved when he smelt a lovely aroma just ahead. Hurrying towards it, he became aware, that it was coming from a house. Now Henry knew that people would be living there, as when the weather was dreadfully cold, his family had sometimes moved into houses to stop them from being frozen. He also knew that if he kept out of their way, he would be safe with warmth, food and water. It was rather cold out here and what was that he could smell? Under the door he squeezed and found himself in the kitchen. This house must have children and these children must have just had their dinner because under the table were bits of peanut butter and dried fruit.

Heaven! Henry ate until his little stomach was fat and round and then he hauled himself onto the table, where there was a cup of water, which he glugged with great satisfaction.

Sliding down the table leg, he thought that he would have a look around. The kitchen cupboards were a food treasure of seeds, nuts, honey and other delicacies. In the vegetable basket were sweet potatoes and he was sure there would be meat and eggs in the fridge, along with half used tins of beans and herbs. If only he could get it open, he would just help himself to a tiny bit that would surely go unnoticed. For now, though, Henry wasn't hungry, so he continued exploring. Next to the kitchen was a room with boxes of toys, books on shelves and stuffed animals. He didn't much like the look of the animals, in particular the fox perched on the armchair or the rubber snake curled up on the soft rug. But in the centre of the room was the most magnificent doll's house, a perfect miniature and just right for Henry's size. He took a deep breath and trotted inside.

It was like a proper house with carpets, wallpaper and curtains. There was even a pretend TV on a swivel stand, lights and pictures on the walls. The furniture was leather with embroidered cushions and there were real, tiny books in the bookcase.

But what amazed Henry the most, was the fully working kitchen with a hob powered by a tea light, water coming out of tiny taps and a fully functioning oven. He couldn't wait to start cooking and spend the night experimenting with all the gadgets, carefully putting them all back in their exact places because he was, after all, an incredibly fastidious mouse.

Over the next few days, Henry's spirits lifted although he was still lonely. During the day he curled up to sleep in a corner of the basement and during the night went searching for fruit in the orchard and collecting food from the kitchen, just a little mind. He had located cookbooks on the shelf in the bookcase in the doll's house and they were proving enormously helpful in teaching him all about boiling, steaming and using an oven. The new tastes were a revelation and he longed to share one of his meals with someone. But Henry did wish that he could get into that fridge, then he could have jam sandwiches, cheese on toast and maybe rice pudding! He was feeling more confident in the kitchen now or perhaps too confident, because one evening as he bent down to take his sweet potatoes out of the oven, disaster struck. He knocked the tea light, the flame caught on his whiskers and they started to burn. Oh, it did hurt, even when he stuck his head under running water in the sink. But even worse, as they dried, they became incredibly brittle and broke off. What was he to do? He would not be able to feel his way around looking for food or go exploring in the garden ... and ... and ... what was that looking at him through the window?

2. Percy and Henry

Percy looked inside the house and there, just a few inches away on the other side of the glass was a sad sight indeed. A little mouse with his whole body shaking uncontrollably and a worried face with bits of stubble where his whiskers should have been.

Percy looked at the little mouse and the little mouse looked back, immobile through fear. But the rat being a sociable animal, quietly reassured the mouse,

'It's ok, don't be frightened. I'm not going to harm you. I am just looking for my family. I'll sit here and you can come out to chat when you are ready.'

Henry was reluctant to come out of the house but Percy waited patiently and eventually Henry's curiosity overcame his fear. He crept out and squeaked,

'H-H-H-Hello, I am H-H'-Henry and I am all alone as well. I am dreadfully sorry but I haven't seen your family.'

'Well, my name is Percy. It's a shame you haven't seen them but where is yours? Why are you on your own? Why don't you tell me all about it?'

So, Henry did, right up to just then when he had burnt all his whiskers off. He felt a lot better afterwards and had almost forgotten about the pain it had caused.

In fact, he was so much more relaxed that he felt brave enough to ask Percy, 'You must have a tale to tell as well. How did you lose your family?'

So, Percy told him about them and how like all rats they are fantastically good at climbing and would collect sticks, twigs and leaves and scramble up tree trunks with them to make a nest. Here, in the uppermost branches they would sleep during the day. He sadly told Henry about last Christmas Eve when it was so cold that they couldn't wait to snuggle down. However, they were woken by a violent shaking movement and the whole tree tipped sideways throwing

Percy out and down onto the ground, where he landed in a heap in a bush. He saw that the tree was now on the back of a lorry that had a picture of a tree on the tailgate, which looked similar to the one that they had been sleeping in, with some writing around it.

Percy had no idea what it all meant or where his family was. He told Henry how he had spent a long time searching and calling for them. Christmas day had arrived and Percy was all alone, scared and exhausted.

I was too petrified to sleep in a tree again,' he related, 'so I settled down in the middle of a pile of leaves for a rest and then continued looking, calling to them from dusk until dawn. I needed water and had to break the ice in the puddles to get some. I needed food but it was difficult to find because of the frozen ground, until I came across an area of land where the soil had been dug and I could see green shoots and leaves growing in rows. There I could dig in the soft earth and feast on green cabbage, crunchy parsnips and tasty spinach.'

'That sounds delicious,' commented Henry.

'It was,' replied Percy, 'until by mistake I ate an onion. I didn't think it was an onion as the frosty air had masked the smell and I ate about half of it. But my stomach can't stand strong tastes like that, so I was awfully ill. I am better now and after having my dinner tonight, I elected to cross the fields on the edge of the wood to see what I could find. I saw this house and thought that my family might be in here for the warmth. I discovered a damaged drain that led into the kitchen, so came in that way. Then I heard some noises nearby.

That must have been when you had your accident. I looked around the door and there you were inside another house. That was extremely surprising to me, so I came into the room to investigate and here I am.'

'Well, here you are and I am glad that you came across me,' replied Henry. 'Can I tempt you with some roasted sweet potato?'

'Well seeing as that's the reason you've lost your whiskers; I think that I had better,' replied Percy. 'But I must warn you that I've never eaten anything cooked before and if it makes my stomach hurt like the onion, I will be vastly unhappy with you.'

3. The Refrigerator

'My word,' spluttered Percy, 'that's a surprise, sweet and soft with a lovely chewy skin. I didn't know that food could be like that.'

Henry just smiled but inside was totally delighted and a little bit relieved.

By now it was almost dawn and Percy needed to find somewhere to sleep. Whilst Henry happily jumped down the cellar steps with a little chirp, Percy perilously clambered up into the uppermost rafters of the house, actually feeling much safer and more content than he had for a long time.

That evening when the two met again, Henry had an idea and leading the way, he took Percy into the kitchen where the refrigerator was standing under the worktop.

Tentatively Henry asked Percy, 'Do you think that you could possibly open that?'

Percy sniffed around looking up and down at the units.

'I'll certainly give it a go,' he replied, as he effortlessly scaled the side of the wooden cupboard that was next to the fridge. 'There, now all I have to do is hold this catch open, shove the top of the door with my nose and hey presto!'

Henry watched as Percy pushed against the door harder and harder thinking that the rat was going to topple over onto the floor. But with one almighty effort the door swung open and Percy was catapulted into the fridge. Then the door banged shut.

Henry stared in terror at the closed door. He called to Percy but there was no reply. He ran around and around in anxious circles. Whatever was he going to do now? It was all his fault that Percy was going to die of the cold. To add to his fear, he heard footsteps coming down the stairs. Skittering across the tiled floor, he hid behind a broom that was leaning against the wall. A lady came into the kitchen and started to open the fridge door. Henry reacted hurriedly and leapt at the broom handle causing it to topple over. As it crashed to the floor and the lady turned to look at what had caused the noise, Percy was able to leap unnoticed out of the fridge and away into the playroom with Henry close on his heels.

'Phew, that was close,' gasped Percy. 'I thought I was going to freeze to death in there.'

'Oh dear, oh dear, I should never have asked you to do that,' spluttered Henry. 'It's far too dangerous.'

'Nonsense. Your quick thinking saved me and I've got the hang of it now. Next time, I'll prop the door open with a tea towel. I'll be right as rain.'… and that's what Percy did.

The meals after that were a culinary delight of tastes, smells and full tummies with Henry and Percy chattering away and becoming firm friends. But they had to be really careful that they took just little bits of foodstuff and not items like whole eggs, which would be noticed. So, one night Henry suggested that maybe the garden would be a good place to visit for different produce. Then he remembered that there was the not so small problem, of him not being able to feel where he was going, because of his missing whiskers. He would likely be some other animal's dinner within minutes, as he would not be able to find cover to protect himself. It was no use Percy going on his own, as he wouldn't know what was good for cooking. What a dilemma. How could they fix it? Would Henry ever be able to go outside?

4. The Garden

Henry looked at Percy, 'You are a large rat with, forgive me, rather large ears.'

Percy looked at Henry, 'Yes, and you are a small mouse who is as light as a feather. Why don't you jump onto my back and nestle behind my ears? I will be your transport and you can be our food and plant expert.'

So, that's what Henry did with Percy carefully meandering around the vegetable patch, being directed towards promising smelling scents.

All of a sudden, in front of them was an expanse of chicken wire.

'Chickens!' squeaked Henry excitedly, nearly falling off his perch and causing Percy to wince, as he screamed in his ear, 'Eggs!'

They began gnawing at the wire and before long had made a hole that was just big enough to squeeze through, being extra cautious that Henry did not tumble to the ground. They swiftly made their way into the chicken coop and there in a dark corner, just a few inches off the floor was a wooden box with half a dozen eggs. Percy gingerly lifted out the smallest egg and passed it to Henry who held firmly on to it. Manoeuvring his way back, carefully negotiating the wire and folding it back into place, Percy had just started to make his way across the garden, when Henry glanced up at the big white moon, which just happened to be illuminating big white wings and outspread talons. He had escaped the owl once and had no intention of becoming the owl's dinner this time.

'Percy! Owl!' he screeched into his ear.

'Hold on tight!' Percy yelled, as he zigzagged in-between the bushes, flowers and trees, jumping over the path and down the house steps. Finally, skidding to a halt at the hole and flinging Henry forward as he nosedived after him. The two friends lay panting with Henry surprisingly still clutching the egg.

He looked at Percy, 'Well, scrambled egg it is then,' and they both burst out laughing with relief.

The garden provided a wealth of interesting and delicious herbs and vegetables. Henry loved being outdoors and was exceedingly comfortable behind Percy's soft, smooth ear, although he had to remember not to shout again.

Another evening they came across a slice of bread and some left-over cheese in the kitchen. Henry thought that wilted spinach would go rather well with melted cheese on toast. Off they went passing the chicken coop and around a corner, where there in front of them was a vegetable patch. Somebody had been really hard at work digging and planting. Henry was so excited that he jumped down and started sniffing around, taking little nibbles here and there, squealing in delight. He located some spinach and asked Percy to dig up a leaf or two. Percy set to work and it wasn't long before he sat back with the shiny green leaves in his paws.

'Is this enough? Henry? Henry?' But however much he called there was no reply. Henry was nowhere to be seen.

5. Corey

Dejectedly Percy trudged back, sitting outside the doll's house holding the spinach, wondering what had happened to Henry. Had he been caught by the owl or was he frantically trying to find his way home? Percy had just made the decision that he really couldn't sit here any longer and had to go and search for him when Henry hurtled into the playroom, closely followed by another little mouse.

'Henry, where have you been? How did you find your way back? Who is that with you?'

'This is Corey,' chuckled Henry. 'Don't look so worried. I'll tell you all about why I was gone so long after we have eaten, as it is way past our meal time.'

Percy had to be content with that and waited tensely whilst Henry prepared cheese on toast on a bed of wilted, especially wilted by now, spinach. Corey seemed relaxed and watched Henry with interest. Soon the three of them were sitting down to the hurriedly prepared meal, which they declared was delicious. After a long drink of refreshing water, Henry began.

'When we were in the vegetable plot and you were digging up the spinach, I was so excited by all the smells and tastes that I wandered away from you, engrossed in all that I could smell and feel. Feel? How was that possible? It was then that I understood that my whiskers had grown back. It had happened so gradually that I hadn't noticed and neither had you Percy! They are still rather soft but they work. I was so thrilled that I ran this way and that way, crossing the meadow, dashing through the trees until I rapidly grasped that I was back at the noisy black field again. That alarmed me and brought me to my senses. I looked around wondering what on earth had possessed me to run so far away from you. I am so sorry Percy.'

'It's ok,' answered Percy, 'I can understand your excitement but what happened next?'

'Well,' continued Henry, 'I was worn out and

anxious, so I uncovered a hollow to rest in. I wanted somewhere safe, until my heart had stopped beating so fast. However, I nearly jumped out of my skin when a voice underneath me said, 'Excuse me, that's my tail you're sitting on.'

'Another mouse was in the hole! That was Corey. Luckily for me, he saw the funny side and after I had apologised, I explained how I came to be there. I couldn't really finish the explanation properly without telling him your story, Percy. Corey said that he was sorry for me but was especially interested about you looking for your family. He thinks it is likely that your family were still in the tree, when it was cut down and not thrown out as you were. Otherwise, they would have surely heard you calling,' finished Henry.

'Yes,' continued Corey. 'I asked Henry, if we could come back to fetch you, as there is something that I think you ought to see.'

'I'm so sorry for worrying you,' resumed Henry. 'I hope that Corey's surprise will make up for it, that is, if you want to go. It is a bit of a trek and it may come to nothing.' Percy was too excited to be angry with Henry and so pleased that his whiskers had grown back, that he agreed to the expedition.

'If there is any chance, that it helps me find my family, then I have to take it,' he declared.

Whilst Percy and Henry were sorting out some provisions to take, Corey was looking around him with delight, 'Superb winter accommodation, Henry. I might join you when the season changes again. If that's ok?'

Henry agreed and then recognised that it was indeed springtime and he ought to be nesting outdoors by now. He had missed being outside and now that he had another friend to share a home with, he should move out of the house.

The three left the house chatting away, getting to know one another. Percy had a good feeling that Corey would be a fine friend for Henry and he was relieved, as he had been itching to continue his search but hadn't wanted to leave him when he couldn't yet fend completely for himself.

Just as dawn was breaking, they arrived at the place where Corey had been nesting and he told

Percy to sit 'just there' at the side of the black field, where he would have a good view.

Percy was puzzled, 'a good view of what?'

As the sun rose, the road, for that is what it was, became busier with vehicles of all descriptions thundering down its straight black strip. It was hurting Percy's ears and he didn't really know what he was supposed to be looking for until 'whoosh' a lorry swooped past with the same picture on the back that he had seen when his family had disappeared. Then there was another, both going the same way.

'What does it mean?' Percy asked.

'They are going to work at the tree plantation,' Corey informed him. 'At Christmas time the trees are loaded on the back to be taken for sale but now it is preparing and planting time, which is why there are no trees loaded on them.'

'Taken for sale!' exclaimed Percy. 'How will I ever find them, if the tree that we had been sleeping in was sold?'

6. The Christmas Tree Plantation

'Ah, but that's the point,' explained Corey, 'after they have been cut down, the trees are stored, waiting to be netted as they are sold. I think that your family will have had time to make their escape out of the tree, before that happened. They might well be living in or near the plantation. Follow the route that the lorries took and you may have a chance of finding them.'

Percy and Henry agreed that it was worth a try and the three of them spent a restless day sleeping, before the sun set and it was time for Percy to go. Percy was elated to be continuing his quest but sad at the same time to be saying goodbye to Henry. For his part Henry was pleased for Percy but also gloomy, that they were parting. The two friends hugged each other warmly. Percy thanked Corey for his help and then he was on his way, walking as close as he could, but not on the road.

He trudged along in the long grass, sometimes having to cross another road to continue following his road. He passed farms with tractors and sheds with broken down cars outside. He avoided going too near buildings and kept a watchful ear for any animal that might like him for their dinner. When daylight came, he slept fitfully, tossing and turning in the unfamiliar surroundings. He plodded on night after night lost in his thoughts. So lost, that as the sun rose and he crossed yet another road, he didn't see the lorry that was bearing down on him until its headlights beamed on the side of his head. There was no time to reach safety. Percy pressed himself down onto the tarmac and closed his eyes. The huge, thundering wheels passed either side of him and as Percy exhaled in relief, he opened his eyes to see a picture of a Christmas tree on the tailgate.

He followed the direction that the lorry had taken and soon came to the yard where it was now parked. There were numerous outhouses, fierce looking machines and some kind of dwelling with a vegetable garden. Percy also distinctly smelled cat. He dashed around in and out of the buildings, calling the names of his parents and siblings. All the time totally aware that there was a cat somewhere. Exhausted, he climbed high into the rafters of a barn and fell fast asleep. In his dreams, there was a cat who was meowing louder and louder. He woke up but he could still hear the noise. He looked around frantically scanning the area until glancing down he saw two kittens play fighting on the dusty ground below. They were tumbling around together and then one would dash off, with the other in hot pursuit. When the first kitten was caught, the game would start again. Percy watched them playing and wondered where their mum was. Maybe she was silently watching as well. He had better wait and see before he emerged from his perch.

The kittens were becoming braver, climbing and jumping with agility. They were even using their sharp claws to climb up the side of a large tub. But when they reached the top, they disappeared with a splash!

'Splash?' thought Percy.

He scrambled down the beams, rushed across the barn floor and was peering into the water butt in seconds. The kittens were desperately trying to grasp the side of the butt, but they were clinging onto each other in fright and getting nowhere. Their terrified meows were causing them to swallow water and it wouldn't be long before they would sink and drown. Percy was a strong swimmer and he dived into the water. Instantly, the kittens grabbed his fur and crawled onto Percy's back whimpering in shock. Their fur was sodden and heavy causing Percy to sink down. He held his breath and pushed his way back up to the surface. The petrified kittens were panicking so much that Percy kept sinking and was becoming extraordinarily tired. Unexpectedly, the weight became less and he saw that an adult cat had grabbed hold of the scruff of one of the kitten's necks and hauled it out of the water. Then repeated the action with the second and soon Percy was able to climb out himself. He lay on the barn floor, utterly spent, breathing hard and looking straight into the eyes of one of his deadliest enemies.

7. Holly and Tinker

For what seemed like minutes but was probably seconds, the cat stared without blinking at Percy. She watched him recover whilst her kittens clambered over him, licking his fur dry. Then she seemed to make up her mind.

'What you did was incredibly brave,' she declared. 'My babies could have died if you hadn't been here to save them. You jumped into the water without a thought for yourself and so I cannot harm you. My name is Holly and I thank you from the bottom of my heart.'

Percy sighed with relief and nudging the kittens away, he stood up.

'My name is Percy,' he replied. 'I am glad that I was here and that your kittens playing woke me from my sleep.'

'You were sleeping?' she commented. 'You don't live here. Are you passing through?'

So, Percy related his story to her, whilst the kittens slept, curled up at his feet.

'Hmm, ' Holly said thoughtfully, 'that's interesting. Now that the kittens have arrived, I don't get out much amongst the trees any more. The furthest I go is into the office, where bowls of food are left for Tinker and me.'

'Tinker?' queried Percy.

'Yes, he's the father of the kittens and well named, as he has sired a couple of real tinkers!' she laughed. 'I should have taken them with me this morning but I couldn't persuade them away from their game. I would never have forgiven myself, if something had happened to them,' she shivered. 'Sometimes it is so hard being a mother.'

'What nonsense,' boomed a gruff male voice, 'easiest job in the world, lying there feeding and preening. You want to try keeping the dogs away from them and guarding our territory from rats and other vermin.'

Percy backed away from the tom cat who was obviously Tinker. Maybe he could just … but too late the kittens woke up and started mewling, causing Tinker to look their way.

'What on earth is that rat doing by my family?' he growled, lowering his body, showing his teeth and getting ready to attack.

Holly sprang between them and as calmly and quickly as she could, explained what had happened. 'Harrumph,' blustered Tinker, 'and just passing through, you say. Well, I suppose I shall have to thank you for saving the little ones from their mother's neglect. Looking for your family, eh? Well, I know this plantation like the back of my paw. Come on, the sooner we find them or don't, the sooner you are out of here.'

So, Percy raised his tired body and trotted along after Tinker, who set off at quite a speed. This was obviously a patrol that he had done many times, sometimes stopping to spray at a fence post or scratch a tree trunk. In and out of the trees they went with Tinker occasionally dashing off in search of a tasty morsel. Percy didn't want to think about that. But he was thinking. He was thinking that these trees were too young and too small for his family to nest in. He promptly stopped and sank to the ground.

'It's no good,' he sighed, 'these trees are not tall enough and anyway, I don't think that they would be happy to sleep again in these kinds of trees, after what happened.'

Tinker glanced at him and even though he didn't want to, he felt sad for Percy. He pushed him to his feet and prodded him in the direction they had come. Percy was so tired and miserable that he wasn't really aware of his surroundings, stumbling along without looking around him. Then just as they were at the entrance to the barn, he let out an almighty howl of pain.

8. Hedgley

Hissing in agony, Percy jumped back and looked down at what had caused such a sharp, intense pain. All he could see was what looked like a ball of needles.

'It's alright Hedgley,' reassured Tinker, 'I know you will think this improbable but the rat is with me.'

Gradually the ball unravelled itself, revealing two dark eyes and the long, pointed nose of a hedgehog. It seemed bizarre to Percy that an animal with such a sweet face could have such vicious spines.

'Well,' laughed Hedgley, 'you do have a habit of making strange friends, don't you?'

Tinker explained to Percy how they had become friends.

'One evening when I was on my rounds, checking that all was well, I came across this hedgehog, (pointing at Hedgley) all entangled in a plastic bag, that had been blown by the wind into the shrubs, where he was resting. I couldn't leave him to die but it took quite some time to disentangle him, what with his sharp needles and my sensitive paws. By the time I had done, we were both enormously hungry, so I suggested that he could share some of my dinner and so, slowly because hedgehogs only have little legs, we made our way to the building where food is left for Holly and me. Hedgley thoroughly enjoyed the chicken flavoured cat food and soon forgot about the danger he had been in.

'Mm,' agreed Hedgley, 'I have a lot to thank Tinker for and that meal was super tasty. Such a treat not to have to hunt for my dinner. Caterpillars, worms and slugs don't come as ready meals,' he chortled.

'Anyway' went on Tinker, 'after that, Hedgley here has taken to regularly turning up to help us eat our cat food. So, not only do I have to guard our home against possible roaming dogs but I often end up escorting him across the yard, looking out for any predatory ferrets or owls.'

At that point Holly came out of the barn and joined in the conversation, 'Stop complaining, you know you love Hedgley's company. You say it's such a change from me chattering about the kittens all the time.'

'Well,' grunted Hedgley, 'I may not be fast and I can't see too well but I have covered a lot of ground in my half a decade and experienced more than your average hedgehog.'

The two kittens now wide awake from the noise and commotion, came bounding outside and started pleading with Hedgley to tell one of his tales. He was only too happy to oblige and the small group of diverse animals settled down inside on the straw for one of his stories.

Hedgley began, 'At just a few weeks old my mother taught us children to forage for such food as worms and beetles. We were supposed to stay close to her until we were older but I was always wandering away. Sometimes she got so annoyed that when she reached me, she picked me up in her mouth, dumped me back in the nest and I would go hungry. But I never learned my lesson. The world was just too exciting and the year too short, as hedgehogs hibernate in the cold winter, so I only had the warmer months to explore.

'On one of my discovering walks, I came across a small pond and thought that I would have a drink, which I did. But the water looked enticing and I was so hot that I opted to have a short swim. I'm a good swimmer like Percy you see. I leapt in and was having a lovely time until I gradually realised that I was drifting down stream. I didn't want to get lost and so I tried to swim to the bank but the current was too strong. It wasn't a pond; it was a river! I was screaming in distress and I kept going under the water.'

At this point in his story, the kittens became overexcited making trilling noises and saying ... 'That was like us, just like us but Percy saved us.'

'Well,' continued Hedgley, 'I was still on my own with no one to save me. Then I hit something hard and clung on. It was the branch of a big tree that was, luckily for me, dangling in the water. I tried to climb onto to it, but I was so tired that my body was trembling and I was so worried that I would drop back into the water. Then something strange happened. It was as if my mum was there but she couldn't be, could she? I was grabbed by my neck, lifted out of the water and plopped down onto the river bank. Leaning over me was a concerned looking squirrel.'

'It's lucky that you're so young with soft spines or I couldn't have done that,' she said softly. 'Now let's get you home.'

Squirrels, unlike hedgehogs, are awfully quick and can climb and jump, so they cover a lot of ground when looking for food. She knew the area well and exactly where our nest was. After an exhilarating journey being carried by her, she deposited me at the paws of my worried mother who had been in tears but was now angrily shaking me.

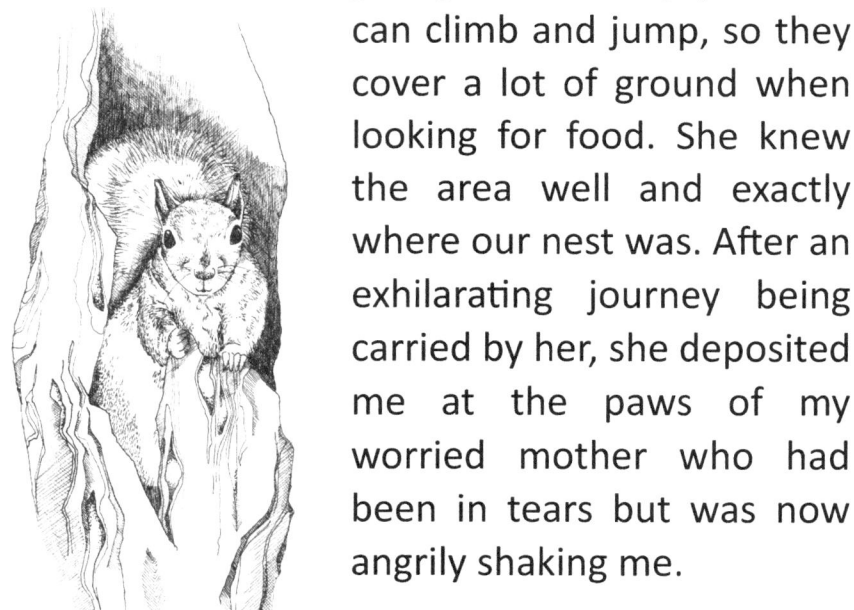

'You have to stay with your brothers and sisters. One day you'll get yourself killed!'

To be honest, the incident had shaken me too but I had gained a good friend, Hazel. We still see each other occasionally when she is in the area. Oh, that gives me an idea. Would you like to meet her?'

'Yes! Yes!' squeaked the kittens. 'Now please, now!'

'Oh no you don't,' interrupted Holly. 'Kittens need their sleep first. It's back to bed for you two. Maybe tomorrow.'

9. Hazel

'You have to be joking,' spluttered Tinker. 'First a rat and now you expect me to welcome a squirrel? It's not natural!'

'Well dear,' soothed Holly. 'If it wasn't for Hazel, you wouldn't have known Hedgley and he has brought lots of joy into your life.'

Tinker didn't know how to reply to that because it was true, but he didn't want to admit it, so he wandered off grumbling to himself. It was actually some days later before Hedgley came across Hazel again. She was nibbling on a piece of bark and looking a little disgruntled.

'I can't wait for the acorns to be ready to eat. They are much better tasting than this and I need to start collecting for the winter,' she explained.

'Well, to take your mind off that you can come and meet some friends of mine,' suggested Hedgley.

Hazel thought that would be lovely, so off they went with Hedgley explaining how he had met Tinker and then the rest of his family. But he did forget to mention one little thing, that was actually pretty important to Hazel. They were at the buildings dotted around the yard when Hazel hissed in Hedgley's ear to stop and stay absolutely still.

'Listen, you'll be safe if you curl up but I am going to have to run up that tree and hide.'

'Whatever for?' responded a shocked Hedgley.

'Don't you see him?' whispered Hazel, 'that big black cat standing guard by the door of the barn?'

'Oh yes, he must be waiting for me. He likes to see that I am safe crossing the yard. I don't know why he didn't come and greet us,' replied Hedgley.

'Well, I am so pleased he didn't,' responded Hazel. 'You do know that cats and squirrels are natural enemies. Why on earth didn't you tell me that your friends were cats?'

'I didn't think it important,' answered Hedgley. 'I just see them as my friends. Oh, and I ought to tell you, that Percy is also staying in the barn for now and he is a rat.'

Hazel rolled her eyes. 'This just keeps getting better and better,' she thought, 'but at least I might have more in common with him.'

Tinker watched from the doorway and fought his instinct to chase the squirrel, whom he guessed was Hazel. Holly came out and rubbed against him reassuringly and lovingly. The kittens bounded over to greet the newcomers with Percy keeping a watchful eye on the proceedings. But as it turned out nobody had needed to worry. The kittens with their relentless inquisitiveness broke the ice and all the animals were soon at ease.

Hazel was told all about Percy's quest and was especially interested as she too nested in trees.

'I think you are right that your family would not want to nest in the fir trees that are on this plantation but there are oaks nearby that are broad and sturdy. In fact, Hedgley, you bumped into one,' she chortled. 'That day you went for a swim, I was by the river checking out one of my favourite trees and you crashed into it!'

Hedgley looked embarrassed but Percy enquired hopefully of Hazel, 'Could you take me to where that is, to see if there any signs of my family?'

Everybody thought that was a good idea and Hazel agreed. Percy was keen not to delay, so although Hazel had only just arrived, it was decided that they should leave immediately. 'We can be properly introduced to Hazel when you return,' pronounced Holly, 'and maybe you'll have some good news.'

After they had left, Hedgley told Holly, that he was feeling peckish, so was just going to look for some slugs.

'Yesterday, I discovered some ditches, where the ground was moist with lots of vegetation. The slugs love that and I had a real feast,' he related.

'Well, ok,' replied Holly, 'but the people don't like slugs eating the vegetables in the garden, so they put down pellets to get rid of them. If you eat a poisoned slug, it will make you incredibly poorly, so be careful and don't be greedy,' she advised.

Meanwhile, Percy and Hazel had arrived at the oaks that were near the river but although they had a thorough search of the area, they did not find anything except for an old cache of Hazel's acorns, which they shared. Hazel said that she knew where there were other oak trees but it would mean them being away for a few days. So, they agreed to go back and tell the others. Chatting away about their intended trip, it wasn't long before they were on the edge of the Christmas tree plantation.

'I think that we should stay in the ditches, away from any eagle-eyed predators,' advised a cautious Percy. Hazel would have preferred being up in the trees but she was happy to keep Percy company.

They were almost back at the yard when Percy gave a yelp.

'Oh no, not again. What has stuck in my paw this time? Hedgley, is that you? What are you doing lying there?'

10. Goodbyes

Hedgley was stretched out on his side, his eyes open with his mouth slightly ajar revealing two rows of tiny sharp teeth. There was no breath coming in or out of that mouth. There was no movement in that tiny chest. The soulful dark eyes were lifeless. Hedgley was dead.

Percy and Hazel looked at one another in shock and then gazed back at the little hedgehog. They stood motionless trying to take in this awful fact. There were no marks on the small body that they could see, so how had he died? He seemed to have been making his way home when he must have collapsed. What on earth had happened? In silent, mutual agreement they carefully picked Hedgley up and took him back to the barn. When they were approaching the yard, Tinker saw them and ran over.

'Is he ill?' he asked.

Then he saw Percy and Hazel's sorrowful expressions.

'Oh no,' he exclaimed. 'Oh no.'

Tinker went inside to break the bad news to Holly and the kittens. After a little while they all trooped miserably outside and gathered around Hedgley.

'I think I know what happened,' said Holly. 'After you two left, he told me that he was going to look for slugs. I think that he probably ate some poisoned ones that had eaten slug pellets and combined with those he ate yesterday, the poison was too much for his tiny body. I warned him that he shouldn't eat too many but he must have done.'

'That's so cruel and so unfair,' exclaimed the kittens.

'Yes,' replied Holly, 'it is very sad and very sudden. I can't quite believe it. We will really miss him.'

The friends clustered around, consoling one another as best they could. Eventually they felt recovered enough to bury Hedgley. They located a cardboard box and after filling it with straw, Tinker carefully lifted him inside. Hazel scratched out a hole under Hedgley's favourite shrub and Percy nudged the box inside. It was left to Holly to say a few words.

'Thank you Hedgley for being our friend. Thank you for all your tales and stories. We will miss you more than we can say but we will always remember you. Goodbye.'

Hazel filled in the hole and the kittens placed some flowers on the grave. It was done. A life was over but Hedgley would never be forgotten.

Percy and Hazel put their trip on hold after this unexpected turn of events. Hazel telling Percy that she would return in a few days and Percy staying to help the others with their grief. He was like a genial uncle with the kittens, playing and consoling them at the times they needed it. Tinker was awfully quiet and held in his grief whilst Holly kept herself busy. They regularly visited Hedgley's grave to reminisce.

The day came though, when Hazel returned and Percy had to say goodbye. It was hard on everyone but they all understood the pull of family. If nothing else the past few days had shown them the strength of the ties of family and friends.

'Good luck,' cried Tinker, Holly and the kittens. 'Come back and see us when you can.'

'I will,' replied Percy, 'and you two little ones don't go giving your mum and dad grey hairs. Stay out of trouble and out of the water!'

Then with a chorus of goodbyes, he and Hazel were on their way.

11. The Oak Trees

There was little conversation as they left the Christmas tree plantation. Hazel felt that she did not want to intrude on Percy's thoughts. He had been through a lot and was setting off into the unknown once again. Walking at a fair pace, the gently rolling landscape would at another time have given them great pleasure but Hedgley was never far from their minds. They crawled under fences that stopped sheep from straying onto the narrow roads and crossed fields of spring barley ready to be harvested. Percy worked out that it must be nearly mid-summer, so he had been looking for his family for more than half a year. If he located his family now, it would only be his mum and dad, as his brothers and sisters would have left home. But he wanted to know that they were okay and he also guessed that they would want to know the same of him.

This thought spurred him on, especially as Hazel said that they were just approaching a wood where there were a number of established oak trees. Percy could see the dense, dark green foliage with some trees having branches that swept the ground and others with trunks wider than the lorry's wheels that had threatened to flatten him. On the edge though was a tree whose massive trunk looked like a giant had split it with an axe.

'That's happened since I was last here,' explained Hazel. 'It must have been hit by lightning in the summer storm that happened here recently.'

Percy was aghast, 'I thought that oak trees were supposed to be safe!'

'They are … mostly,' responded Hazel.

They meandered into the wood with Percy calling out for his parents and Hazel keeping a lookout for predators. Unexpectedly there was a tremendous chattering and squawking, as a cloud of starlings raised the alarm.

'Hurry,' hissed Hazel to Percy, 'climb up this tree and hide in the branches at the top.'

Percy didn't wait to be told twice and quick as a

flash they were peering down through the branches to see what had upset the birds. It was blurred down on the ground for Percy, but Hazel had exceptionally keen eyesight and when her body stiffened Percy knew she had seen something. Prowling through the vegetation was a fox with its rusty red bushy tail scraping the woodland earth, two upturned, pointed ears and a snout sniffing the air. They froze, hardly daring to breathe. The fox walked slowly around their tree and with its excellent hearing Hazel was sure that they would be discovered. It seemed like hours later but was really only minutes when the fox moved on and Hazel was able to tell Percy that they were safe … for now. They both let out huge sighs of relief.

Hazel commented, 'If it hadn't been for the starlings' warning call, things could have been very different. I think that we've had enough excitement for now and he might return, so we should rest here, for a while.'

Percy was only too happy to agree and they settled down into the leaves.

As the sun set, they climbed down from their lofty perch and continued the search. But after a couple of hours and finding nothing, Hazel could see that Percy was becoming dreadfully despondent.

'I have an idea,' she said. 'Not too far from here is a famous oak tree. It is about 500 years old and 12 metres high. Some people think that it possesses magical powers. Maybe, in some way, it could help us find your parents. What do you think?'

Percy was happy to agree, as he was keen to see such a remarkable tree. They set off at a quick pace with Hazel describing how the tree was just outside a tiny village, on the side of a hill. They had been walking for an hour or so when they both sensed that something wasn't right.

They could see an orange light ahead that was nothing to do with the golden fields they were walking through. Then they could hear people's voices and see lots of movement. But what was most concerning of all was that they could feel heat.

12. Chief

The tree was on fire! Orange flames were enveloping its trunk, whilst red hot sparks flew up into the air. Percy and Hazel stood watching in silent amazement and consternation. A dozen firefighters were blasting tonnes of water from long fire hoses snaking the ground. But by the time the fire was out, the tree had been reduced to smoking, charred remains. Gone was the historic, gnarled old oak that every Summer Solstice had been adorned with trinkets, ribbons and flags. The magic powers it might have had were not enough to save it. Sadly, Percy and Hazel walked on, not really knowing where they were going anymore.

The unexpected loss of the tree shocked them and Percy in particular was already especially aware of how quickly life could change. He sniffed the air. In amongst the traces of smoke, there was something else, something that alerted him to an animal presence. What was it? He didn't feel threatened. The smell was stronger now, much stronger. Then in the dawn light, he noticed a pair of ears popping up out of the grass. Then another and another.

'Rabbits,' he said to Hazel.

They stopped and watched the young rabbits, as they jumped up into the air, twisting and spinning themselves around again and again, often falling over in the process. It was hard not to smile at their playfulness and soon Percy and Hazel were laughing aloud at their antics.

This must have alerted the mother rabbits who had been cleaning the nests nearby, for they appeared and began to nudge their offspring home for their daily feed.

Percy and Hazel could now see that they were on the edge of a large field populated by caravans and tents. The holidaymakers would be asleep they guessed but not for much longer and the duo needed to find somewhere safe to rest.

As the sun rose, they were approached by a rather large male rabbit. 'Thought I'd come over and see if you needed assistance,' explained the rabbit. 'You two look rather lost and tired.'

'Oh, yes please,' replied Percy. 'We have come a long way and had a bit of a shock. My name is Percy and this is Hazel.'

'Pleased to make your acquaintance. You can call me Chief, as I tend to rule things around here. I know it might be a bit unusual but if you like, you can rest in our warren until you are recovered,' suggested Chief.

Percy and Hazel were more than happy to accept his offer and followed Chief as he led them to the well-hidden entrance. There they rested and at dusk came above ground and watched the young rabbits playing again.

'You don't want to stay around here for long,' Chief warned them. 'The tourists bring their dogs and if they slip their leads, they love to chase us rabbits and I guess they would you as well. We have a complex burrow system to escape them but you wouldn't know about that. A few weeks ago, I had to warn a couple of rats about them. We have been in this field for ages, long before the campers. And they are only here for a few weeks of the year.'

Percy was hardly listening to Chief's chatter as he absorbed what the rabbit had just said.

'Chief,' interrupted Percy, 'did the rats say why they were here?'

'Well,' replied Chief, 'they were keen to be on their way, as they were looking for somewhere safe to make their home. Seems that they had had some trouble in the past.'

Percy could hardly contain the excitement that was bubbling up inside him.

'It's my mum and dad. It has to be! Where did they go?'

'Well, like I said, I told them about the dogs and they weren't happy about that, so they left pretty sharpish. They went off in the direction of the castle. Lovely place it is with a deer park, lake and lots of trees.'

Percy had to cut in on Chief's description again, to ask him exactly where the castle was.

'Oh, it's not too far. You can almost see it from here just beyond the lake. I'll walk with you a while and tell you some more about it,' said the talkative rabbit.

Chief continued to chatter, with Hazel politely listening whilst Percy was eager to increase their walking pace, his eyes boggling with anticipation and grinding his teeth with excitement. He didn't notice Hazel twitching her tail, as she spotted something that appeared threatening in the corner of her vision. But Chief had seen the warning flick and knew that danger was nearby.

13. The Lake

'Right, listen,' Chief swiftly instructed, 'lay low and I'll grab the dog's attention away from you. Good luck.'

'You too,' answered Percy and Hazel, 'and thank you. Maybe we will meet again one day.'

Through the long grass, they watched the white of Chief's tail as he zigzagged across the field, drawing the large, barking dog away from them. They hoped he would be safe but he seemed confident enough and was practised at outwitting dogs.

So, now they were left to find the castle without their guide. They kept moving in the same direction as before until they became rather tired. There were a few trees ahead of assorted types and sizes and they sat down to rest at the foot of one that offered some shade and protection. The weary friends were dozing when they became aware of something flicking in and out of their vision. Percy and Hazel kept absolutely still and the shadowy shapes transformed into delicate, spotted bodies with long elegant legs. There were six of them, some grazing, others acrobatically leaping around looking for food. Munching, moving, munching, moving. Never staying still, showing their white rumps as they bounded through the trees. Percy and Hazel watched transfixed, as the deer began to move away from them.

'We should follow them,' commented Hazel. 'After all that eating, they will need to drink, so there's a chance that they could lead us to the lake.'

So quickly and quietly, that is what they did. Percy stayed on the ground and Hazel took the upper route of the trees, so that they wouldn't lose sight of the deer. It was Hazel who first saw the water and scrambled down to tell Percy.

'Oh, good,' said Percy, 'the deer aren't the only ones who are thirsty.'

By the time Percy and Hazel made it to the lake, the deer had gone but they could see the tops of the ramparts of the castle. Having satisfied their thirst, they sat back and listened to the weir as it tumbled and crashed down the concrete overflow. Sitting on the edge was a smallish animal with large, protruding eyes and a greeny-brown scaly skin.

It was sitting stock-still and as they watched, its long tongue swooped out of its mouth catching an insect on the end. It then closed its mouth, gave a huge swallow and blinked hard, causing its eyeballs to disappear into its head for a moment. Then it did the same thing again and again, enjoying a hearty meal. Percy and Hazel were so amused at the toad's way of eating and couldn't stop themselves from bursting out laughing. They clutched their stomachs with tears of laughter streaming down their faces.

'Excuse me,' thundered the annoyed toad, 'you are disturbing my dinner with your noise.'

But the more they tried to stop, the more they giggled. The toad stared at them, not understanding what they were laughing about. Eventually becoming so angry, it puffed itself up to appear larger in an attempt to frighten them away. But this looked so comical to Percy and Hazel, it caused them to laugh even harder. In disgust the toad turned his back and hopped into the long grass, presumably to find somewhere quieter to finish its dinner.

Wiping their eyes, Percy and Hazel felt a little ashamed of themselves for upsetting the toad. But unwittingly its behaviours had lightened their mood and they carried on far more cheerfully. They passed a children's play area and headed towards the fluttering flags of the castle. Soon they came upon some open grassland and now that they were out of the trees, the sky could be seen more clearly. As they gazed up, they could see small pools of turquoise gradually being covered by darkening clouds. The trees in the wood ahead seemed to be silhouetted against the sky and all was unnaturally still and quiet. The friends felt a strong sense of foreboding in the air.

14. The Storm

Suddenly a wind started to blow, quickly becoming blustery with drops of rain falling onto the dry ground. Clips of lightening highlighted the dark clouds followed by a low grumbling, rumbling sound. The clouds were growing into the size of mountains and abruptly unleashed a torrential downpour onto Percy and Hazel. An almighty thunderclap caused them to jump out of their skins and run towards the shelter of the trees. But once there Percy became extremely agitated.

'I just don't like this,' he cried, 'after my experience of a falling tree and the one we saw that was hit by lightning.'

'Keep on running,' panted Hazel.

So, that's what they did and after a few moments, they came upon a cave-like structure nestling in the side of a small hill. There was a partially open wooden door at the entrance which they quickly pushed past and threw themselves into the dim, cold but thankfully dry interior. 'Phew,' gasped Hazel, 'summer storms really take you by surprise.'

'I don't think that I like surprises,' wheezed Percy.

'And … we don't like trespassers,' exclaimed a voice from above.

Looking up they could see two large, dumpy birds. The one who had spoken to them and another who was shyly hiding behind.

'My name is Sid,' said the first wood pigeon, 'and this is Cindy. We have made our roost in this old ice house and don't intend sharing, so please leave.'

'Hello,' replied Percy. 'My name is Percy and this is Hazel. Please don't worry, we have no intention of staying for long. We are only sheltering from the storm and then we will be on our way. Hazel is helping me with my quest, you see.'

Sid looked at them beadily. 'Quest?' he queried. 'What quest?'

So, Percy told him his long tale, right up to escaping from the storm, which was even now raging overhead.

'Hmm,' said Sid thoughtfully, 'so you think that your parents might be living in the castle?'

'I hope so,' answered Percy. 'Our separating was so sudden and unexpected. They don't know what happened to me and I don't know what happened to them.'

'Yes,' replied Sid, glancing at Cindy who was still tucked in behind his feathers, 'I can see how upsetting that would be. Maybe I can help you. I have many relatives living up at the castle and I could ask around if any of them have seen your parents.'

'Oh, that would be amazing, thank you,' enthused Percy.

As soon as the storm had abated and Percy had given descriptions of his parents, Sid was as good as his word and flew off to make his investigations. Cindy went with him, as she was far too shy to stay on her own with Percy and Hazel. The two of them were sitting at the entrance of the ice house, looking at the newly soaked ground, when both were amazed to see hopping past ... the toad!

'Not you two again,' it croaked, turning away from them.

'Oh, please stop,' called Hazel. 'We are so pleased to see you, as we wanted to say how sorry we are for upsetting you. It was wrong of us to laugh at you. We are really very, very sorry.'

'Harrumph,' grumbled the toad, peering closely at them and then seeing how ashamed they both looked, replied, 'I accept your apology but I really must be on my way. I hear that there is a wedding up at the castle and I rather hope that they will be having a BBQ. I do love a bit of cooked meat every now and then.'

'Yes,' replied Percy, thinking of Henry, 'I know what you mean.'

Giving Percy a puzzled look, the toad hopped away.

'It was really lucky that we bumped into him again,' said Percy, 'I was feeling very guilty about upsetting his feelings.'

'Yes,' agreed Hazel, 'me too. Although your comment about cooked food puzzled him.'

Percy laughed, 'I know but I do think that this might turn out to be our lucky day.'

Percy was proved right ... up to a point.

A short time later, Sid and Cindy returned with news from the castle.

'Do you want the good news or the bad news?' Sid asked.

'Oh, good please,' replied Percy eagerly.

'Well,' Sid continued, 'it appears that two rats matching the descriptions you gave me have recently been nesting in the attics. They turned up a few days ago, so it is very likely to be them.'

'Oh! Oh! Oh!' squealed Percy jumping up and down with excitement. 'Take me there! Take me there! Why are you waiting?' he added, as Sid didn't move.

'There's a problem,' replied Sid sadly, 'that's the bad news.'

15. The Ending

Sid told them that he had learned that the owners of the castle were having a lot more bookings for weddings and conferences for large groups of people. So, they were busy making improvements and one of these was to convert the attics into bedrooms and bathrooms.

'The building people found that many rats and pigeons had made their homes up there,' he continued, 'so a firm has been employed to rat and pigeon proof those areas and put down traps.'

'I met many of my relatives leaving, as they have experienced this before and know that they should depart as soon as possible. Your parents aren't used to living in houses and won't know the danger that they are in.'

'Well, we have to tell them … quickly … we must go,' exclaimed Percy.

'Yes,' agreed Sid, 'but the firm may already be

blocking the entry pipes that the rats like to use, because then they are not seen. You may not be able to get in or if you do, you may not be able to get out. You could be trapped.'

Percy thought about the danger, but said he was willing to take his chances.

'Oh dear,' muttered Sid, 'I really didn't want to tell you the very bad news. There's a wedding going on.'

'Yes, yes, I know,' exclaimed an exasperated Percy. 'The toad told us. I know there will be many people.'

'But what you don't know,' went on Sid, 'is that there is to be a falconry display at the wedding.'

Percy and Hazel looked at each other. They knew that falconry displays used hawks and they knew what hawks like to catch and they knew that that was … them!

'I have to take the risk but I don't want anyone else to,' Percy stated looking at Hazel.

Hazel argued with him but Percy was not budging

in his opinion, so reluctantly agreed that she would wait by the castle walls.

So, the four of them set off, with Sid and Cindy showing the way. When they made it to the dry moat, Percy continued on his own. Crossing the large, deep ditch, he could see all the cars that were parked in front of the imposing, old building. There must be hundreds of people, he thought, and some of them wouldn't like rats at all, so he would have to be very careful not to be seen. He entered the quadrangle and cautiously skirted the edge until he came to the walls of the castle. Then he looked up to where Sid had told him that the two rats had been seen. It was a long climb but he would try and get up there by using the drainpipe.

So, that's what he did, clambering into the thankfully, not blocked pipe and scrambling up until he arrived at the guttering. Sniffing around, he came across a hole in the eaves and ... there he was ... inside the attics! Very, very cautiously he moved around calling as he went. But he was terrified that he would be caught in a trap, causing his body to shake and his voice to be weak. The attics were dark, dusty and dreadfully depressing. Percy was so dejected that he crumpled down in a heap and started to sob. It was just all too much for him.

'Percy? Percy? Is that you?' he heard and as he looked up, there to his utmost surprise and intense joy was his mother and, incredibly behind her, his father.

'I heard you crying,' his mother explained, 'a mother never forgets their child's cry.'

The reunion was all that he had hoped and longed for and as they hugged and kissed, Percy started to tell them about all the months of searching.

'Oh dear,' he said abruptly stopping. 'We have to leave before our safe exit is blocked.'

Percy's mum and dad looked at him curiously, baffled about what he meant, but seeing how agitated he was, quickly followed him. He led them back the way that he had come until they got to the drainpipe.

'Look,' said Percy, 'we had better go down one by one in case there is an obstruction at the bottom. I'll go first and let you know.'

So, off he went, only to have his fears confirmed, as the exit and freedom was now full of some kind of mesh that he couldn't push through.

'Oh dear, oh dear,' thought Percy, making his way back up the pipe again. At the top, he explained to his mum and dad that they were going to have to risk leaving more openly.

'There are a lot of people out there but don't be scared. You'll be fine if you stay close to me. Once outside, I know where I am going.' He resolved not to tell them about the bird display.

First, they had to navigate their way from the attic, down through all the floors. Fortunately, Percy's mum and dad knew where the first flight of stairs was located. Once they had accomplished that, without setting off any traps, the descent was fairly straight forward. The three rats travelled down and down keeping close to the walls and listening for anything that might pose a threat. Happily, the castle was deserted, as everyone was outside celebrating the wedding or involved with the BBQ. They made their way to the main door which had been left ajar for the guests to use. Percy peeked outside … .and there in the middle of the quadrangle was a crowd of well-dressed people all watching the display, which to Percy's dismay had not yet finished. He did not tell his parents for fear of panicking them. 'Well, at least the people have their backs to us,' he thought.

'Right, mum and dad, we are going to have to run to where my friends are waiting. Follow me.'

So, that's what they did but they had only gone a few metres when there were shouts of alarm. The falconry display was not going as planned. The hawk had seen the three rats and unable to resist his nature was ignoring the lure that the trainer was holding and heading like an arrow straight for them! It swooped over the people's heads and as it began its dive to the rats, the audience ducked and turned away from the hawk's sharp beak and talons. As they did so, some of the crowd saw the rats and began to scream and scatter. It was mayhem with people shrieking and running all over the place. In the commotion the hawk lost sight of the rats giving them a chance of escape. They ran between and around legs, across the quadrangle and underneath the food tables, surprisingly bumping into a bewildered toad eating his BBQ'd meat.

'Toad, quickly come with us in case the hawk sees you,' gasped Percy.

A confused toad, who had been too pre-occupied with his food to notice anything else, hopped along after them and they all collapsed into the dry moat where Hazel, Sid and Cindy were anxiously waiting.

'Well,' commented the toad dryly, after he had recovered his breath 'that's another dinner you've ruined for me.'

Chortling happily and relieved at the end of the day's adventure, the animals trooped back to the ice house where Sid and Cindy were now surprisingly welcoming hosts. After a few days of rest and Percy's parents catching up with all that had happened during his quest, it was time for Percy's parents to look for a winter home. Percy determined that he would go with them to make sure that they were settled somewhere safe.

Again, sad 'goodbyes' had to be said but Percy would never forget any of the animals that had helped him succeed in his quest to find his parents and achieve a happy ending.